How Paul Trained Men

How Paul Trained Men

Gene Edwards

SeedSowers Publishing
Jacksonville, Florida

How Paul Trained Men

Copyright © 2007 by Gene Edwards

Printed in the United States of America
All rights reserved

Published by: SeedSowers Publishing
                P.O. Box 3317, Jacksonville, FL 32206
                800-228-2665
                www.seedsowers.com

Edwards, Gene
How Paul Trained Men
ISBN 10: 0-9778033-6-8
ISBN 13: 978-0-9778033-6-1
1. Seminaries—church planters—first-century church—Paul of Tarsus

Times New Roman 13pt

ALSO BY GENE EDWARDS

THE CHRONICLES OF HEAVEN
Christ Before Creation
The Beginning
The Escape
The Birth
The Triumph
The Return

THE FIRST-CENTURY DIARIES
The Silas Diary
The Titus Diary
The Timothy Diary
The Priscilla Diary
The Gaius Diary

INTRODUCTION TO THE DEEPER CHRISTIAN LIFE
Living by the Highest Life
The Secret to the Christian Life
The Inward Journey

Paul's Way of Training Workers or the Seminary's Way
The Shocking Story of the History of Bible Study
Why You Should Consider Leaving the Pastorate
The Organic Church vs The "New Testament" Church
Problems and Solutions in a House Church
How to Start a House Church From Scratch
Why So Many House Churches Fail and What to Do About It
The Christian Woman . . . Set Free
Beyond Radical
The Divine Romance
A Tale of Three Kings
The Prisoner in the Third Cell
Letters to a Devastated Christian
Exquisite Agony
Dear Lillian
Climb the Highest Mountain
Revolution, The Story of the Early Church
How to Meet in Homes
The Day I Was Crucified as Told by Jesus the Christ
Your Lord Is a Blue Collar Worker

CHAPTER ONE

Eight Men

We all know about the twelve men Jesus trained. They traveled with Him for about three years. But do you know the *eight* men Paul trained? He, too, had men travel with him... men he trained.

Paul's way was remarkably similar to the way Jesus raised up men. Unfortunately, a flat-surface, one-dimensional study of the New Testament will not reveal this. You will not find Paul's way of training or the men being trained if you read Paul's letters in the order you find them in your New Testament. You must read Paul's letters in the order he wrote them. It is then that these eight men practically jump off the pages, and you see them everywhere!

What you are about to read is *not* for everyone. We must tread carefully, as most men are not ready to break with today's seminary way of training, and they should not. The training of men in Century One and today's training are mutually exclusive.

Meet the Eight

Let us meet the eight men trained by Paul: Titus, Timothy, Gaius, Aristarchus, Secundus, Sopater, Tychicus, and Trophemus.* You have read these *names* before, but a traditional, flat, one-dimensional Bible study cannot reveal these men and their roles. It takes context and reading Paul's letters in the order in which he wrote them.

WHY THESE MEN?

Jesus trained twelve men. These men were Jews and would not have been enthusiastically going out and preaching Christ to heathen Gentiles. It would take being struck down by the blinding light of God to get just one Jew to do this. God needed *Gentile* workers to raise up churches in a Gentile world. It was that one Jew who gave the world Gentile church planters.

It was these eight men who went out preaching Christ where His name was not known. You may have noticed their names when reading your New Testament, but the arrangement of Paul's letters (as read today) do not aid us in seeing these men fully. The eight catch our attention only as we read the New Testament *chronologically*, with historical context, times, dates, places, and in alignment with Acts, when applicable. It is then that these men emerge onto the stage . . . front and center. They become very visible, in letter after letter.

If you are a Gentile, these men have played a key role in your salvation. Looking at church history in reverse, you see these men taking Christ to *us* non-Jews. We meet the eight *before* we meet the apostles. Yes, these men came after the Twelve, yet the eight belong to the

---

*Later the eight were joined by Epaphroditus, who went by the name Epaphras in Asia Minor and Epaphroditus in Greece.

same era as the apostles. It is these men who brought Christ to us in Europe and Asia Minor. Keep in mind that when we meet these men, we are meeting the *Gentile* expression of the church.

The Twelve were with Jesus. The eight never met Jesus. They came *after* He had ascended. What does this mean? We look to these eight men to discover how men are trained *after* Jesus ascended! It also means it is to the eight we look to see how men should be trained today.

Ephesus

From which church did each of the eight men come? What were the qualifications required before coming to be trained in Ephesus? When did they arrive? How long before they began training?

What previous experiences (including persecution) did each man know in the church from which he came? What are their backgrounds and culture? What language do each of them speak? Why did they all convene at Ephesus?

Again, our present, one-dimensional Bible study cannot answer these questions. In fact, these questions are not even considered today! But with chronology, the answers to these questions spring forth...along with the story.

Let us now face one of the most important questions of the faith.

How are men to be trained now that the Lord is not physically present on the earth? Seminaries? Surely not. It flies in the face of all reason. (Not to mention the fact that there is no scriptural basis for today's seminary method!) The answer is found in the life of a church planter named Paul. It was Paul's way of training men that has become our North Star. (That was a long time before the man-made invention of seminaries. Nor do the two bear any resemblance.)

What qualifications did these men have in order to be trained by Paul? What was Paul looking for in these young men?

In order to enter most evangelical seminaries, you must have a letter from your pastor. Not so with the Twelve or the eight. The qualifications for these men fit nowhere in today's concepts of training!

These eight men arrived in Ephesus and remained for nearly three years, but that was not the beginning of their training. Their training had begun in church life before they arrived in Ephesus. They each had met *crucial* experiential qualifications *before* they walked through the gates of Ephesus.

CHAPTER TWO

QUALIFICATIONS...
FIRST-CENTURY STYLE

All eight men had previously lived in church life before arriving in Ephesus. And some church life it was! Living in the daily experience of church life was part of both qualification and training. This is qualification *one*!

A CALLING?

Did each man have a call from God? Unbelievably, we do not know, except for Timothy. The rest? Either called or compelled by revelation of Christ and the church.

APPROVED IN FULL VIEW OF THEIR CHURCH

Each man's local gathering (who knew him utterly) approved him. Then he packed, left home, and set out for Asia Minor.

WHO TRAINED THEM?

They were then trained by an *old* church planter, a church planter with lots of church life experience. Nor did Paul train these men the way men called of God today are trained (Preaching 101, Systematic Theology 101, etc.).

After Training Ended

There is also another world we rarely consider. What did these men do *after* the training ended?

What Did the Eight Do Next?

Actually, what these eight men did after training was an *extension* of their training. Training did not end after the men departed Ephesus. The answer to that question is something which *must* be restored. Know the answer to that question and you will even find the ultimate purpose of training, of being a worker, a co-worker, and even discipleship!

Have you been called of God? Have you be drawn by a revelation of Christ and the church? Are you desperate for a spiritual life that goes far beyond your own present state?

Do you know what you have been called to *do*? Today's approach to the way men are trained for the Lord's work does not fit that calling! For some, your calling is not to be a pastor of a church. After all, the modern-day practice of the pastorate is extra-biblical, invented during the Reformation. (Honest!)

There was a first-century *way* of training men, and that training fit a first-century *calling*. As the story unfolds, this incredible way of training emerges as nothing less than awesome. Truly it is the kind of training only God could think up!

Let us get to know these men Paul trained. We will commence with the first man to appear on the stage. We will meet him in full dimension. (By the way, it appears his brother or uncle did not like him.)

CHAPTER THREE

TITUS, THE FIRST TO BE QUALIFIED

His name is Titus. He appears in the story before Timothy.‡ His home was in the capital of Syria...Antioch. He was Greek. He was one hundred percent Hellenized (Greekized). His culture was Greek. His gods were Greek. His language was Greek. His haircut was Greek. His education was Greek. Titus was a heathen!!

In order to better know Titus, let us estimate his age. This can aid us by giving a sense of the passing of time. (True, we do not know his actual age, but by establishing an age, we can watch Titus move through time for the next 40 years.* If you prefer a different age, please use your own estimate.)

What were Titus's qualifications for ending up in Ephesus? How was he trained? The answers are beautiful when seen in the context of the church! Not to mention being revolutionary!

It is possible that Barnabas raised up the church in Antioch. If not, at the very least he greatly aided the Antioch

---

‡ Timothy appears in about the year 48. Titus appears as early as the year 43.
* We estimate Titus to be 4 years old on the Day of Pentecost, making him 17 or 18 in 43/44 when Paul arrived in Antioch with Barnabas from Cilicia.

church in its early years! Among those who gathered in that ekklesia was a young, uncircumcised Greek: Enter Titus!†

Given the chance, would you choose the experiential training Titus received or going to a seminary?

TITUS IN THE YEAR 43

In 43 Titus is seventeen. Mark this: Titus witnessed the beginning of the church in Antioch. He was more or less "there from the beginning." Titus entered into the *daily* experience of the life and adventures of the Antioch church.

Whatever you have read of the church in Antioch, as told by Luke in Acts, Titus saw it! Titus entered into and began experiencing something called *church life* . . . that is, the outliving of the ekklesia day after day. (The term church life is *not* a reference to today's traditional way of having church.)

It is there in Antioch that Titus gained one of the ingredients which later qualified him to be trained. You cannot give what you have not previously experienced. Having been in church life for a good period of time is qualification *number one*. Titus had *church life* in his own experience to draw from. He did not read about it. He lived it!

This was only the beginning of Titus's remarkable journey. Consider all that happened in Antioch! What a church it was to experience!

Early on, Titus sat at the feet of Barnabas and heard him tell tales of the Day of Pentecost and the wonders

---

† Did he have a brother or uncle studying to be a doctor? If so, we have real reason to believe that this doctor-later-turned-author did not like Titus.

of the early church which followed. Titus heard firsthand all about everything covered in Acts1:1 to 13:1.

Because Titus was present when the church was born, he saw the "how" of raising up the church by watching Barnabas. Titus knew the man who knew the apostles. (Titus later met all the apostles.) Some background for a kid of 17! Some ingredients for training!

Titus, a Gentile Christian, was in Antioch when Barnabas arrived with Paul. That must have been quite a moment for the church, considering Paul's reputation as a former persecutor of the church. Titus lived in close proximity to Barnabas and Paul from 43 to 47. He also knew Simeon called Niger. He knew Lucius of Cyrene and Manaen. Titus also heard about the prayer meeting where five men who, while ministering to the Lord, heard the Holy Spirit separate Paul and Barnabas to be sent out to the Gentiles. Titus was present when Barnabas and Paul left Syria (in 47) for Cyprus and then Galatia. Later, Titus was in that awesome meeting when Barnabas and Paul returned home to Antioch (in 49) and told the church their story of their two years' journey *and* the planting of four Gentile churches way up there in someplace called Galatia...an astonishing tale indeed. Titus heard not only how the Lord opened the door to the Gentiles, but also the grizzly travel conditions, the beatings, the stoning, and the rejection.

He also heard of the time John Mark left Paul and Barnabas at Pamphylia and returned home to Jerusalem. Shortly after that report, lo and behold, Peter came to Antioch to visit the church (in the year 50). Titus witnessed the commotion and turmoil in the church caused by the (Christian) Pharisees who had come from Jerusalem, demanding that *he* (and all Gentiles) be circumcised and observe the Law of Moses.

Titus was there, front and center, when Paul rebuked Peter... in front of the church! That is a pretty large slice of *pre*-training right there! (By the way, church life is still tempestuous.)

Titus was most likely overwhelmed when *he* discovered that he was selected by the Antioch church (Paul even said by revelation) to go to Jerusalem. He was to go with Paul and Barnabas to meet with the Twelve and there to work out the problems caused by the legalistic visitors who had come to Antioch from Jerusalem. Titus, in Jerusalem, was an eyewitness to the very serious issue of salvation by Christ only or salvation by Christ plus. This very heathen-looking (and uncircumcised) young Greek also met with the Jerusalem church, the Twelve, and John Mark. Titus was a living, walking, breathing embodiment of the issue at hand: Should Titus and his kin be cut with a knife?!

Titus watched Paul and Barnabas stand nose-to-nose with the Pharisees and give up not even an inch to anything they said. He must have stood breathless as he witnessed the Jerusalem letter being dictated by James and Peter. It must have been a heart-stopper as he then watched, dumb-founded, as the Twelve, then the Jerusalem elders, then Silas, then Paul and Barnabas signed that letter (in the year 50). And when the quill was handed to him, I speculate he probably just about fainted. (I would have.)

Titus returned to Antioch. On the way, he came to know John Mark! (The man Peter calls Marcus my son.) Did not Titus inundate John Mark with questions? After all, here was a young man, only slightly older than he, who had heard and seen the Lord. He knew of the death of James, the deliverance of Peter out of jail, and he was on part of Paul's first journey.

("Come on, John Mark, write some of this down and make me a copy.") Then Titus witnessed Paul and Barnabas having a falling out because of John Mark. Here is more rock-bottom reality available only in church life.

Titus, like the fifty million other people living in the Roman Empire, heard that the Emperor Claudius had ordered all Jews (about 20,000) out of Rome in late 49. Titus was there in Antioch when Paul learned about the Judaizers who had tried to wreck the Antioch church and from there had traveled all the way to Galatia to destroy those four new churches. (This invasion was taking place while Paul and Barnabas were in Jerusalem.) Titus was right there in the room when Paul actually penned the Galatian letter! Titus watched the very first piece of Christian literature being written. But, more important to Titus than all of the above, he was asked to deliver the Galatian letter to the Galatian churches (Galatians 2:3). This was summer of the year 50.

Now we have Titus traveling alone, delivering the Galatian letter to four churches in a land he had never seen. Paul would arrive shortly after Titus reached Galatia, and he would have Silas in tow. (No wonder Paul did not bother to mention the Jerusalem letter; he just let the two witnesses tell the story.)

Having delivered the letter to Galatia . . . ah . . . what happened next? Titus returned home to Antioch and continued on in that wondrous, hair-raising experience called *church life*. Or is it possible that Titus was on Paul's second journey? We will never know because Luke never mentioned Titus. It was as though Titus never existed. All that we know of Titus we learn from Paul's letters. After Acts 13:1, Titus is there in the events recorded in Acts, but he is *never* mentioned in Acts! Why? Did Luke, the physician turned historian, really dislike Titus that much? Or . . . ?

This we do know, Titus lived in the raw realities of church life—Christians caught up in the drama of what *church* was really like.

This, dear Christian reader, is step one in first-century style training for future church planters! This training is for the body of Christ. Such training can only be found in the daily outliving of the church. Would you prefer less?

At that time, in the spring of the year 50, Titus was age 24.

Pass through and survive church life and you will be a man, my son, fit to go on to the *next* step!

Now we come to the second of those eight men. Here is where the fun really starts.

We will leave Titus for a little while, but pick up with him again when he meets this second man.

CHAPTER FOUR

TIMOTHY'S QUALIFICATIONS

When Barnabas and Paul were on that *first* church planting journey, they met a young, very overlookable kid! He was living in one of the four cities where Paul planted a church.

It was in Lystra that Paul met a half-breed (half Jew, half Greek). Though Luke did not mention this boy as he recorded Paul's first time in Lystra, the lad was there. So were the boy's mother and grandmother. The young man's name was Timothy. The year Paul first entered Lystra was the year 48. We will estimate Timothy's age to be twenty in the year 48.

Let us look closely at this future co-worker to Paul and close friend of Titus.*

Timothy witnessed the "how" of raising up a church by watching Paul. Once more, we have a man "there from the beginning" . . . the beginning of a church.

Timothy saw Paul being stoned and left for dead. (Seeing your mentor stoned is a good introduction to what life is like for men who serve Christ outside the institutional church.) Timothy watched Paul leave Lystra

---

* If Titus actually delivered the Galatian letter before Paul and Silas arrived, then Timothy and Titus met. Perhaps not, but perhaps!

and Pisidia *and* Iconium *and* Derbe. He also saw a band of Pharisaic legalists come as pretentious visitors from Jerusalem with a letter from James the brother of Jesus. It is almost at the exact time that Paul is stoned in Lystra—where Paul had met Timothy—that the third man of the eight arrives on the scene. His experience and Timothy's experience merge!

CHAPTER FIVE

ENTER GAIUS

It is still 48. Paul leaves Lystra and travels to Derbe. We will give Gaius the age of twenty-five in A.D. 48. What do we learn of Gaius? He was there at the birth of the church in Derbe ("there from the beginning"). Also, Paul spent less time in Derbe than any other ekklesia. At some point, Gaius and Timothy met one another, as Lystra and Derbe were close (84 miles). Gaius was there when Paul left the church in Derbe... left the church all on its own. Not long after that, early in the year 50, Gaius was the first to meet the Judaizers from Jerusalem. Because the Judaizers came by land, they arrived at the city of Derbe first. Derbe was probably the least prepared to handle those men with "another gospel." Gaius saw these legalistic men attempt to defame Paul and to convert or destroy the four Gentile churches. Gaius, like Timothy, saw the four churches pass through a reign of confusion.‡

It was on Paul's second journey (in the summer of 50) that Gaius met Silas. We can say that up to this point, Gaius and Timothy's experiences were virtually identical.

---

‡ Gaius also watched Timothy walk up to those Judaizers—face to face—confronting them in all four churches.

The two young men heard Paul report about the church in Antioch, about the legalistic Jews' visit there, and of the gathering in Jerusalem of all the apostles. Timothy and Gaius filled Paul in on the details about these same Judaizers' visit to Galatia and how Timothy went head-to-head with them. Silas was there with Paul and told his version of the Jerusalem Council. The two men also saw Silas unroll a letter signed by all of the Twelve.

After Paul visited Lystra and Derbe on his second journey, things changed. Paul circumcised Timothy. Does that mean Gaius had inferior qualifications? No. Never forget, just being in church life is a qualification within itself! Also, while Gaius was with Silas, be sure he and Timothy plied Silas with questions. As we leave Gaius, we will give him the age of twenty-six. We will meet him again in Ephesus, with Timothy and Titus (even though the beloved physician refused to mention him).

Dear reader, envy those young men. And yes, church life is still that exciting, not to mention tempestuous, if not downright dangerous!

Paul and Silas left Galatia in late 50 and continued on their way.*

---

* It is very possible Titus is also with Paul. We will never know because Luke—in Acts—never mentions Titus being there; in fact, Luke *never* mentions Titus, ever. Scholars believe Luke either disliked Titus intently or, far more likely, Luke was the older brother of Titus, and did not want to be found presenting his younger brother in a good light. There are two men often present in this saga recorded in Acts: Neither of them are mentioned in Acts. They are Luke *and* Titus. *It is only* in Paul's letters that we find three men mentioned in these events. The conclusion is obvious. The men who left Galatia in 50 were possibly Silas, Timothy and Titus. We will never know. Luke, why did you leave Titus out of everything you wrote?

Timothy was twenty in the year 48; he is now twenty-two. Be impressed. Timothy had stood up to the Judaizers at age twenty-two!

A Glance at These Three

Unless single brothers have greatly changed, those three men (Titus, Timothy, and Gaius) quizzed Silas for every detail of his life! *And* of one another!

Learn, then, why experiencing *church life* in your locale . . . in your life *before* being trained . . . is so important. (Again, this is not a reference to modern church life).

The one unique ingredient of Ephesus was that a man was present who was totally outside all old religious tradition and who was a weather-beaten old church planter with two decades of church planting and even more years of church life.

As Paul, Silas and Timothy set out on the *second* journey, Gaius continues his experience of church life in Derbe. (Titus is either back in his home church in Antioch or with Timothy on journey two. We will never know. Luke, why? Historians are not supposed to be prejudiced.)

Timothy, Paul and Silas eventually headed out for Greece with Timothy walking between two men whose experience dates back to Pentecost, to the Twelve, and to Barnabas. Timothy also walks between two men who were at another huge event, the Jerusalem council. Timothy also learned the perils of travel in that age. That is important. How do men handle the rigors of travel and long periods of time from home and families? This is one of the best measures of men there is. (*Stay-at-homers* are not cut out for this job of church planters.)

Did Silas tell Timothy what it was like at Solomon's Portico, of Stephen, Aristarchus, Phillip?

We now prepare to meet the next three future church planters. All were born in the small country of Greece.

IN THE MEANTIME, UP IN GREECE[†]

In late 49, the Emperor Claudius ordered all Jews out of Rome. There were thirteen districts in the city of Rome. The people in Philippi (Greece) looked upon themselves as the fourteenth district in *Rome*. The people of Philippi—a Greek city—spoke Latin, they wrote Latin, their money was Latin, so were their clothes, customs and their architecture. Further, they *were* citizens of the city of Rome, made possible by a decree of Augustus.

By late 50, the Philippians had run every Jew out of the city limits.

Ironically, in the year 50, Paul and Silas—both Jews—arrive in Philippi! Timothy, you will recall, had seen Paul stoned in Lystra. Now he watched Paul beaten (with Roman rods) in Philippi. Timothy also saw Paul and Silas thrown in jail and then shackled.

Next, Timothy watched two men rejected by an entire city. This is excellent training for a young man entering the Lord's work.

You need church life first-century style if you aspire to be trained first-century style.

True church life is not easy to come by! You may have to look for it.

[†] If we are ever to understand our New Testament, we need to pay attention to surrounding major events.

All the men who were trained in Ephesus had known church life before they were trained.

CHAPTER SIX

THESSALONICA GIVES USTWO MORE MEN

After leaving Philippi, the three men move south to the capital of Macedonia in northern Greece. Paul enters the city of Thessalonica in the year 51.‡

They are now about to encounter two more future workers... in one church.

ENTER ARISTARCHUS AND SECUNDUS

When Paul raised up the Thessalonian church, among the converts were two future church planters. They are number four and number five (of eight). The names of these men are Aristarchus and Secundus. Both were Greeks. Again we see that prospective church planters had been "there from the beginning." These two men came to know not only Paul and Silas, but also Timothy as well. (Plus Titus? We do not know.)

These two men were there "from the beginning," and it is important that they saw the *how* of the birth and growth of an ekklesia.

---

‡ I feel certain Titus was with Paul by this time. The words "we" begin to appear in Acts. Luke is letting us know that he himself is present, but does not use his own name. If Luke is present, can Titus be far behind?

The church in Thessalonica had a hallmark. They seemed to revel in persecution. They loved to hear stories about how the church in Jerusalem was persecuted... probably along with the stories told by Silas! This church also seemed to have a vivid imagination when it came to eschatology.

Aristarchus and Secundus probably saw Paul's beaten and scarred back. They watched Paul being forced out of the city by an assortment of local citizens, government officials, and Jews. Nonetheless, this Gentile ekklesia seemed to enjoy persecution and social rejection. Before the persecution began, if we know anything about enthusiastic single brothers, these two young Greek men pumped Silas and Timothy with many a question.

One night the two listened to Paul tell about a riot in Rome led by Jews who believed that if Paul led a revolt in Rome, the Jewish Messiah would appear in Rome and would overthrow the Romans. The coming Messiah did not come. Instead, Claudius ordered all Jews out of Rome. From that day on, the Jews considered Claudius to be the anti-anointed one (an anti-messiah).

Aristarchus and Secundus' journey in church life began in persecution. They entered into a tumultuous life at the very outset.

The entire city hated this Christian presence. Further, in Century One, church life and adventure were one and the same.

A few weeks after their conversion, these two men not only found themselves in a group of believers surrounded by rejection from government, citizens, and Jews, but at that very time, Paul left them on their own during those hair-raising days. Paul left the church all alone. Paul was an example to these two young men by life, by word and, later, by his letters.

Just as Titus had seen the birth of a church in Antioch, Timothy a church in Lystra, and Gaius a church in Derbe, these two men, Aristarchus and Secundus, had a ringside seat at the birth of a church *and* living in church life right in the midst of persecution. And *then* these two men and their church were left alone!

It is the year 51.

We will estimate these two men to be age twenty-five in the year 51.

By now, Gaius has seen Paul leave Derbe; and Aristarchus and Secundus have seen Paul leave Thessalonica.

At this point, Timothy has seen Paul leave *six* churches.[*]

---

[*] Acts 14:23...they (Paul and Barnabas) commended them to the Lord in whom they had believed. They dared to leave each church to the care of the Holy Spirit!

CHAPTER SEVEN

ENTER BEREA AND A YOUNG JEW!

The story of the birth of the church in Berea is almost a duplicate of what happened in Thessalonica. One reason for this is the fact that some Thessalonians came to Berea to stir up trouble. The other reason is that the two cities were geographically close.

In Berea, there seemed to be a good number of Jews in the synagogue who were converted to Christ. These converts managed to gain access to the synagogue's Hebrew scrolls. Each Saturday they requested certain passages be read to them. (*Jews* were supposed to hear these readings. The Gentile converts were not ever allowed in the same room.) A priest unrolled the Hebrew scroll and he read the requested passages.

One convert was Sopater, a Jew.

Sopater, too, was "there from the beginning." He entered into the boiling pot of church life which was there in Berea from virtually the outset of the church's beginning.

In the year 51, we will give Sopater the age of twenty-five.

Timothy has seen Paul leave the church in Philippi, Thessalonica, and now Berea. Timothy and Aristarchus and Secundus watch as Paul leaves Thessalonica!

Paul is still averaging being with a church less than six months per church. Will there ever be such men who will *dare* to follow this divine habit?

Paul leaves Berea in great haste. "The brothers" escorted Paul to Athens. (Was Sopater one of those brothers?) Paul stayed in Athens about a month, while Silas and Timothy stayed in the Thessalonica/Berea area. Later they came to Athens and gave Paul a report on the status of the churches in Philippi, Thessalonica and Berea.

After that, Paul moved on to Corinth. Once in Corinth, he heard a second report about the churches in Thessalonica.

What Paul heard caused him to write a letter to this exuberant and persecuted church. (Who delivered the letter to Thessalonica? We will never know.) Aristarchus and Secundus were present in the meeting when Paul's letter was read to their church. By mirroring (inverting) that letter, you will be able to gather an idea of what had recently happened in the church there.

After Paul sent his letter, he had Timothy revisit the church in Thessalonica. Aristarchus and Secundus had a ringside seat to watch all that happened in the Thessalonica story. Again, if we know *anything* about single brothers, the two men once more plied Timothy with yet more questions. Among other things, they wanted to know what happened in Athens and Corinth. Timothy, in turn, inquired as to how the church in Berea was doing.

There is no question that Aristarchus and Secundus had visited the Berean assembly. Paul instructed Timothy to stay in Thessalonica, with Silas in Berea. This gave Aristarchus, Secundus, and Sopater two men to pummel with questions.

You will notice their training was not from out of a book.

Paul in Corinth

Paul had left these churches he raised up in Greece—left each church within four to six months. Paul now had six possible future workers. And he had plans. Big plans.

CHAPTER EIGHT

PAUL RETURNS HOME—WITH PLANS

Unlike the other cities Paul visited, he was in Corinth for eighteen months.

But he still *left* the church in Corinth. Paul, Silas, and Timothy all left Corinth and, with a quick stop in Ephesus, they then journeyed to Jerusalem and the church there. Do not overlook this: Timothy was with Paul and Silas when their second journey ended. It ended in Jerusalem, and Timothy was there.

Timothy visited the church in Jerusalem in 54. Titus had been in Jerusalem in 49.

THAT BRIEF STOP IN EPHESUS

Before going to Jerusalem, Paul had made a side stop at the famous city of Ephesus. He asked Aquila and Priscilla to move there. Paul had plans. Later, there in Ephesus, Paul would one day train men to raise up churches.

After a short visit in Ephesus, Paul and Timothy visited Jerusalem and there bade goodbye to Silas. Timothy and Paul set out for Antioch where Paul reported on his second church planting journey.

Timothy has now seen the Antioch church.

(Did Timothy meet Titus for the first time, or was it that he and Titus had already traveled together?) What was the "church count" for Timothy? So far, four Galatian churches—Philippi, Thessalonica, Berea, Corinth; a glimpse of Ephesus and the church in Jerusalem; and now Antioch.

And all we offer young men are four walls of a seminary! You thought you had only one choice for your training . . . may I suggest that you have another!

Very soon at Ephesus, you will observe something no seminary will ever afford—the greatest cross-pollination of spiritual experience and practical church experience in all history. Paul wrote a letter to the Galatian churches, including the two home churches of Timothy and Gaius, Lystra and Derbe. He then wrote a letter to Thessalonica. (We can be sure this letter was read in Berea, which was just up the road.) Paul asked each church to send a specific man: a brother from Derbe, two from Thessalonica and one from Berea. He did not send a letter to Antioch because he was in Antioch at the time with Timothy and Titus at his side. The message was the same to each brother: Leave your city and meet me in Ephesus. So it was, dear reader, that it came to pass that *six* young men set out for Ephesus. Those six men soon arrived in Ephesus. Collectively they had "seen it all." They saw an experienced church planter raise up churches. More than that: They saw his life given to and for the churches. They saw Paul's life poured out for the churches. Then they watched Paul leave the churches in the care of the One they believed in! What a Lord Paul had! What a Lord he gave the churches!

It is the year 54.

By that year, the Daggermen, started in Galilee in 52, were trying to find Paul. Also in 54, Claudius died. A sixteen-year-old boy by the name of Germanicus Nero ascended to the throne as ruler of the empire.

There is a strong possibility that Paul had thought that just maybe Germanicus *would* lift the ban against Jews living in Rome. His mother Agrippina was known to be sympathetic to the Jews.

The sixteen-year-old Nero—and the aging Paul—have fourteen years left to live. Paul will spend at least six of those fourteen years in jail, while Nero will be living a fantasy that belongs only to a madman. After all, Nero was the nephew of mad Caligula!

While Paul trained men in Ephesus, he also kept a close eye on Nero, hoping the young emperor would allow the Jews to return to Rome. If so, Paul would go there. If not, Paul had a plan to circumvent the ban. One way or the other, Paul was determined to be the person who first planted a Gentile expression of the ekklesia in Rome.

The Ephesian Line of Churches

When Paul created the concept of the Ephesian line, it was pure divine genius. It was soon thereafter that Paul came up with another divine concept: how to plant a church in Rome (a city without a single Jew in it), and how to be the one who would plant it. The Gentile version of *transplanting* a church would be Paul's way of shipping a full grown, *complete* church all the way to Rome!

In a multi-dimensional (historical, cultural, political, biblical) view, Paul's letters are aligned with Acts 15:40

through Acts 18. This view cannot be seen in a one-dimensional Bible study. Verses sewn to other verses (out of context and not in chronological order) cannot compare to a multi-dimensional look at the Scriptures.

What you have read so far is not today's seminary education, is it? Nor can a seminary compete with this way of raising up men called of God.

Dear ones, we have been hoodwinked through the centuries into believing that formal schooling is required! Reread Acts and Paul's letters. See the drama... feel the ebb and flow of life. Watch these men plant churches... and then leave. How could a seminary education possibly replace such a God-given pattern?

CHAPTER NINE

THE MIRACLE THAT HAPPENED IN EPHESUS

Six men arrived in Ephesus from six different cities, each bringing six different cultures, languages, customs, geography, and governments. They met in a setting foreign to *all* of them! Nonetheless, consider what each man can bequeath to the other five.

Titus can tell the other five all about Barnabas, Paul, Antioch, the Peter-Paul confrontation, the Jerusalem Council, the Twelve, Silas and the Jerusalem letter, and Paul's letter to the Galatians about the invasion of the legalists.

Timothy can tell just about *anything* about Lystra, Pisidia, Iconium, Derbe, Philippi, Thessalonica, Berea, Athens, Corinth, a brief trip to Ephesus, *his* own trip to Jerusalem, and Antioch. Timothy can also tell them all about the hazards of traveling in places all over the empire, what it is like trying to keep up with the audacious, tireless Paul, and about the beatings, jailing, stoning, and whipping that Paul endured. He can tell them just about anything that has do with Silas, and anything else they might want to know, anywhere, any place!

Aristarchus, Secundus, and Sopater can tell them about living in Greece and the Greek world, about the

Greek churches, the Greek mind, their visiting the ekklesia in Philippi and the tumultuous time in Corinth, and what it was like to live in a sea of social rejection in Thessalonica for years.

And you? All you have is seminary.

It is the year 55. The ages of these men? Titus is thirty-two. Timothy is twenty-eight. Gaius is thirty. The three Greeks (Aristarchus, Secundus, and Sopater) are all twenty-eight.

All of these men have had experiences of seeing the birth of *at least* one church. Each man can stand up and say "I was there from the beginning." (The Twelve could say the same thing.)

Soon, they will *all* be able to say it . . . *twice*.

THE BIRTH OF THE CHURCH IN EPHESUS

The eyes of these six men watched Paul raise up the body of Christ in the city of Ephesus. Those six men, all who were at the beginning of the ekklesia in their home city, now watch Paul nurture the young church in Ephesus for the next three years.

What a beginning! Even Timothy must have been impressed. (See Acts 20–21.)

All six could now say, "I was there from the beginning . . . two times."

And what will you be able to say after years of sitting in class taking notes from your professor?

We now watch the *six* become the eight!

CHAPTER TEN

FROM SIX MEN TO EIGHT

Even before these six men passed through the city gates of Ephesus, Paul began the church in Ephesus. How? In a most amazing way. He met twelve followers of John the Baptist. (John had long since died, in 27 or 28. This was the year 54, over 20 years later.) Paul baptized all twelve of these men. When the six arrived, Paul marched into the city of Ephesus... with twenty men (the eight plus twelve) as the beginning of the church in Ephesus.

Among those twelve converts were two men (most likely biological brothers) named Tychicus and Trophemus. These two men did what all first-century believers did: They entered into both *salvation* and *church life* simultaneously.

Three years later these two men, Tychicus and Trophemus, became church planters in the kingdom.

So it came about that the six men Paul had trained actually turned out eventually to be the eight!

Eight men were trained.
Eight men were sent.
Jesus trained twelve. Jesus sent twelve.
The Holy Spirit sent Barnabas and Paul.
What of the six? The six were sent by *the church*. But never fail to add that it is when we see those passages

that describe Paul's trials, ordeals and physical sufferings do we realize what these men experienced with Paul. This life is what Paul passed on to those eight men, along with the daily experiences of living in the church. These men were trained by a beat-up old itinerant church planter.

Each man's story was a little different from the others, but Tychicus and Trophemus were unique. These two men experienced church life *and* were in training *at the same time*. They were trained in the same place where they had been converted, and in a brief amount of time.

This way of training is so utterly different from the seminary. Why? One reason is that the original premise of the seminary is flawed.

CHAPTER ELEVEN

AFTER EPHESUS, THE NINTH MAN

While Paul was living in Ephesus, it appears he led a young man to Christ whose name was Epaphras. Epaphras was from Asia Minor, but not from Ephesus. Epaphras came from a small village called Colossae, located ninety miles east of Ephesus. This remarkable man later became a church planter, and later even a co-worker of Paul's. Epaphras turned out to be an amazing man. He became number *nine* to be trained! But more than a co-worker, Paul out-and-out called Epaphras an apostle!§ (Our Bible translations—perhaps under the influence of John Darby—refuse to properly translate the word that Paul used to describe Epaphras.) In Greek, Paul called Epaphras an *apostle*. Other translations call him "an ambassador." There are more than just the Twelve plus Barnabas and Paul who are *sent ones*. Sirs, why not allow Epaphras to be what he is? After all, Epaphras raised up three churches. These three churches, all near to one another, were Colossae, Hierapolis, and Laodicea. Further, when Paul wanted to go to Europe, to Philippi, but could not, he sent Epaphras, a man from a village in

---

§ Philippians 2:25.

Asia Minor, to take his place to help the church in Philippi. Paul asked Epaphras to be the one to become the apostle to Philippi.

So it is, we ultimately had nine young Gentile church planters to carry on Paul's work.

Did the training end after Ephesus? And what did these men do after they departed from Ephesus?

CHAPTER TWELVE

WHAT WAS PAUL'S WAY OF TRAINING MEN IN EPHESUS LIKE?

The training in Ephesus, what was it like? (Like a seminary?) And after Ephesus, what happened?

Let us hope Paul told them of his life. That would probably do more for them than we could imagine. It is the way men lived during crises that matters to young Christian workers. (Look through Paul's letters: he had plenty of crises to deal with!)

But let us go to the hallmark of his words. Paul knew of and spoke of that which had to do with other realms. He always had an other-realm gospel which centered on Jesus Christ.

Let us hope he taught them practical solutions which he had found for a menagerie of problems. Certainly there was experience enough in that room concerning the raising up of churches. (Dare we say he spoke of the eccentricities of God's people?) He explained how to survive persecution and its effect, externally and internally, and come out neither bitter nor damaged.

Paul taught them to lose, which is perhaps the greatest of all lessons to learn in the endless challenges of church planting. Eight men saw Paul's own words in *action*. That was training enough. Add in the Holy Spirit and the indwelling Lord, and Paul gave that which, in modern terms, cannot be given: He gave them a spiritual life, a Christ-centered matrix. Paul spoke to those men of matters which seminaries know little and practice even less.

Paul presents Christ to those men! A living, breathing knowledge of Christ. Should you question that, then reread his thirteen letters. Their centrality is Christ. He gave them divine encounter. What Paul gave those men was an infusion of his own life, which was "to live is Christ."

Never forget, these men watched Paul raise up the church *and* nurture the church. Those were spiritual churches he raised up. He did not suddenly become a man of methodology.

Paul drew from his experience and then passed that wisdom, born in fire, on to them. He gave these men a lifetime of church life, church planting and the Cross. They noticed that at the core of it all, he had the constant words "know Christ, know nothing but Christ."

He probably gave them some hard-earned advice about travel—on oceans, *in* oceans, bandits, betrayal, rivers, storms, rats, and lice. This is not a classroom setting, nor captivating pulpit oratory. Paul gave them suffering. He showed them the cost of the daily living by Christ. Paul's way of training was in two words, *Paul's life*. Paul's training was *Christ*.

Paul gave these eight men the *centrality* of Christ in all things and the centrality of Christ in the ekklesia.

PAUL WAS A CHURCH MAN

Paul did something else that is lost to us. He raised up church men. And, in his consistent habit, he also *left* them.

The Cross which Paul gave them was the cross of first-hand experience, not a book nor a theory. The Cross, by the way, is *loss*, not gain.

DID PAUL TEACH THE BIBLE?

The seminary teaches the Bible as so centralized, and as the solution to all things, that this singular approach almost leaves out the centrality of Christ in all things. It comes close to establishing the Bible as central in all things.

Keep this in mind always: The only part of the New Testament that existed in 54–58 was Galatians, I Thessalonians and II Thessalonians; and that, dear ones, was all Paul had penned. What of the Old Testament? With the possible exception of Timothy, none of these men could read Hebrew. *No*, the Old Testament in Greek was not available to these *uncircumcised* unwashed, unclean heathen.

We of the twenty-first century are only now beginning to understand how rare it was for a synagogue to have a complete Old Testament. And all copies—presumably less than fifty copies anywhere in the world—were in a language called *old* Hebrew, a language no longer spoken at that time. Be sure, no Gentile, nor Paul, could get their hands on a complete Old Testament. It would have been unlikely to ever see the Torah in a Jewish synagogue there in Ephesus.

Paul did share aspects of the Old Testament and did so by means of the time-honored *oral tradition*. And all that he gave them of the Old Testament was the Christ of the Old Testament . . . as you see reflected in Paul's letters.

PAUL AND THE EIGHT MEN IN THE MARKETPLACE

Eight men had a ringside seat to watch Paul as he worked with the church in Ephesus . . . and as he worked with his hands in the marketplace repairing tents. This was on-the-job training at its best.

CHAPTER THIRTEEN

NEXT, PAUL SENT THOSE MEN OUT INTO ASIA MINOR

While still in Ephesus, Paul sent these men out to nearby towns in Asia Minor. That is, Paul engaged in a high compound of on-the-job, local, apprentice-type training coupled with "turn them loose and let them practice."

Some of the churches which John later mentioned in Revelation were raised up by these eight men.

AFTER EPHESUS

Paul then went farther. Paul kept on training these *eight* men after their time in Ephesus ended. This, in fact, may have been the most important part of their training.

Let us discover what happened after the training. Would you believe he took them as tourists to Jerusalem (the eight meeting the Twelve)?

CHAPTER FOURTEEN

AFTER THE TRAINING ENDED

Paul gave the eight a tour of the Holy City. In fact, Paul's arriving in Jerusalem with the eight ended Paul's public ministry. When the training in Ephesus ended, Paul took the eight men with him to Philippi, and then to the port city of Dyrrachium (today Durres) in western Greece, just across from Italy. There at Durres, they turned north for a brief journey into Dalmatia. They then came back to Philippi in Greece and on down to Corinth. There Paul wrote to the Christians gathering in Rome! What he did next might be the same anyone might wish to do today. He took the eight men on to Jerusalem.* (The year is 57–58.)

After his arrest in Jerusalem, the record of Acts tells us Paul sent some of these eight men out into Asia Minor, Greece and Italy.** Meanwhile, Aristarchus and Luke stayed with Paul where he was in prison in Caesarea. Aristarchus later accompanied Paul the prisoner on his journey to Rome.

---

* Perhaps to avoid their being charged with the one charge made against Paul, that he had never been to the church in Jerusalem, Paul brought these men to Jerusalem.
** Back in Israel, John Mark was writing the first biography of the life of Jesus Christ (A.D. 55–56).

It strongly appears Luke was in Rome with Paul. Luke appears to have been writing the Gospel of Luke and starting the book of Acts, either in Caesarea or Rome.

During the last days of Paul's life, these men, including Epaphras and even John Mark, along with Titus and Timothy, came to be with Paul in Rome.*

From the year 58 to 68, we surmise these men did what they were trained to do, strengthen existing churches and plant new churches.

Today we await the return of the itinerant church planter, the start-a-church-and-leave-it church planter—a Christ-centered man outside the religious traditions of his day.

---

* You will see all this clearly, but *only* if you follow Paul's letters in the order in which he wrote them.

CHAPTER FIFTEEN

HOW THESE MEN WERE *NOT* TRAINED

THIS IS THE KEY TO TRAINING

These men received training that did not resemble the Plato/Aristotle/cubicle lecture room/sit-and-take-notes which typifies today's seminary. Why have we settled for such a low-realm, frontal-lobe way of training men?

True, every professor in a seminary is a hero to someone in that seminary; but when we look at Paul's life, the life of our seminary professors pales in comparison.

The eight sat at the feet of one of the most despised men of their era. What else is there about this man?

OUR GREATEST MISTAKE

Perhaps the greatest and most universal mistake we Christians make concerning the training of men is the unconscious assumption that teaching men the Scripture is the total of what training is.** Learn the Bible and presto! you are trained and you are also qualified!

** Trust me, dear reader, as one who has trained men according to what you are reading here, integrity ranks above all else. It is not Greek, not education, not spiritual power, nor exegetical insight, nor even oratory abilities.

Paul's way shows us a far, far broader view than "teach them the Bible, and let them go," which is essentially the Bible school way of doing things.

Come to the seminary for several years, learn the Bible (by sitting in a chair in a cubical), and then walk across a stage, receive a certificate. *That* is all it takes for men to be trained!

Paul became involved! These eight men observed Paul's life. They heard his experiences. Paul himself was always part of their curriculum. So was their own experience of church life in Ephesus. Church life Paul's way was the content of their daily life and training.

Let there be a few daring souls who are not satisfied with the current training methods. Let there be those who seek the church as she was in her early days . . . free and functioning. And then, let there be those who wish to live in such church life!

CHAPTER SIXTEEN

WHO IS QUALIFIED TO DO THE TRAINING?

A beat-up old man who did one thing... he planted churches. (He also did a little writing!) He did the training. No one else. A sunburned, blue collar worker. A man hated. Loved. Revered. Despised. Lied about beyond all telling, yet as true to his calling as realities can afford. As Theodore Roosevelt observed, it is not the spectator, nor theorist, nor critic, nor lecturer, but "the man in the arena... bloodied and bruised." Only those men and *those men alone* know true success and true failure.

I wonder: Could any man be truly trained unless he sat under a man despised? What good would it do, otherwise?

If the eight had questions, Paul had answers!

He, in turn, trained the men to do what he did. He was a master builder, a church planter (of the kind of churches of that day, not the kind of churches of our day). These eight men did not pastor nor do anything similar to what seminaries produce.

We would be hard pressed to successfully justify the existence of *any* training that took place in the New Testament era other than that of raising up *church planters*.

Repeat: All callings in the New Testament era pointed in only one direction: called to plant churches. (Not to plant *a* church and then stay there!) Might this be your calling? Your *only* calling?*

If so, seminary may not be . . . !!

Is there any kind of calling in the New Testament other than *being a church planter?* I know of no other. Mark this: it is the kind of church planter whose hallmark was/is to plant churches and then *leave*, with occasional return visits. It is the most visible kind of church planter recorded in Century One, be it the apostles, Paul, Barnabas, or any others.

Is there a chance you were called to such a walk? Only one question remains. Are you *willing*, even daring . . . because in this day, daring is a necessity. That is, are you willing to leave the institutional church and its mindset? If you cannot understand that question, you do not understand the task to which you are called. If the answer is *yes*, then it might be wise for you to begin looking for a beat-up old church planter who has lived his entire ministry "outside the box," a man who will give you Christ with just about every breath he takes!

You want to go to a seminary? You want to learn to be a pastor (a position that never existed before the Reformation)?

If you *want* to be a pastor, by all means go to the seminary.

On the other hand, the prototype we are seeing was an old church planter who had a passion for non-legalistic ways. He was a man *outside* the box. If you had lived

---

* "But I feel called to teach in a Bible school." That is pretty good, to be called to a non-biblical, non-existent calling!

in Century One and you were looking for such a man, you might have decided against its being Paul... too many horrible rumors about that man! If you cannot be trained by such a beat-up old man, then either 1) go to seminary, if that is satisfactory to you, or 2) if no such man exists, start a revolution—a revolution that leaves the box and leaves it forever. For yourself, though, do not train men until you are a beat-up old church planter yourself, one who has planted freedom-steeped churches. Churches which, after you planted them, you left, and they continued on. Churches which have lasted despite the fact they were born and raised in the whirlwind of persecution! Churches where everyone functions, and what they speak and what they know is Christ. Churches where no whiff of sacerdotalism exists, and elder, elders, and elder*ship* are never discussed!**

And be sure that the man who trains you is not salaried—that he works with his hands in order to earn his own living.

That should not be too hard to find, should it?

We will close by looking at how the eight died.

** Please see *The Organic Church*, SeedSowers Publishing House.

CHAPTER SEVENTEEN

WHAT HAPPENED TO THESE MEN?

You know how life ended for Paul, but how did the eight/nine die?

THE FIRST TO DIE WAS...

Secular history gives an accounting of the fate of Aristarchus. He was the first of the nine to die. He died in the year 64, at the hands of Nero, burned as a torch to light Nero's garden. The other men? If church tradition can be trusted, they all died violently.

PAUL

Paul's *public* ministry ended when he was arrested in Jerusalem in the year 58.* After that, the eight men watched Nero's attempt to destroy the Christians in Rome. They also saw Israel sink into civil war (65–66). They watched 60,000 Roman soldiers march on Israel,

---

* A man who looked like the Gentile Trophemus was the cause of Paul's imprisonment in Jerusalem. Then came Paul's imprisonment in Caesarea, followed by his imprisonment in Rome. That is a period stretching from 58 to 63. By 66, Paul was in prison again, and by 68 Paul was dead.

and news later reached them that Jerusalem had been destroyed (August of the year 70).

After Paul died, those of the eight who were still alive became the men who continued taking the Gentile gospel and raising up Gentile churches.

How Did the Rest Die?

Was John Mark pulled apart by wild horses? Did Timothy die in Asia Minor and Titus on Cypress? Did Epaphras die in Philippi? Sopater in Rome? This is what tradition tells us.

Gaius's death is unknown to us, so also the death of Secundus.

There is another way to die. Most men in the ministry superannuate from the pulpit and then begin drawing their denomination's pension until they die. That is the "other way" to die.

On the other hand, there are a few who do not feel that is an appropriate way for a minister of the gospel to die. It is for these men this book is written. They will move as Paul moved, raising up churches where Christ is all in all and God's people function in every meeting and live in freedom.

———•·•———

We have come to the end, and now it is time for you to make a decision.

If you have read to this point and are content to take your training in a seminary, then by all means, do so. Join the ranks of the vast majority.

Sir, if you can take the seminary route, you have earned the right to all that institutionalized Christianity is waiting to bestow on you!

But, if you absolutely cannot go that way, then you might want to ask around to see if anyone knows of a man—he will not be in the institutional church—not even remotely—who is still alive who has a medallion around his neck.

A medallion?

Yes, I placed that medallion around that young man's neck in my old age. Further, that medallion is engraved with an *electric chair* on it. On the reverse side are the words "Die Daily."

Be sure to ask him how it came to be that he possesses that medallion, and what it cost him in years and tears.

Perhaps his answer will be that he received that medallion in the remote Waldensian valleys, located high up in the northern Italian Alps. That medallion is his equivalent of another man's MDiv. . . . and much, much more. Be sure, he either paid with "blood" to wear that medallion, or he watched an old man who did.

Why the Waldensian mountains? Because long, long ago there were a people called the Waldensians who regularly sent out men to plant churches across Europe. They did so in the darkest days of the Dark Ages. In those days, so long past, before the Waldenses sent out their church planters, they first held a funeral for the one they were sending. Why? Because those Waldensians knew they would never see the worker again, nor know where he fell. So it was that they held the funerals of those men, knowing of their certain death and in places of which they would never know.

Young man, young woman, your heart should seek no lower standard for your calling! What shall you do if the man who wore that medallion died long ago? Then look around. There are a few things about God we can predict. He will raise up another man not to dissimilar from the men who came before.* Find him. Follow him. Or be him.

God give us such men... for whom Christ is their magnificent obsession... and Lord, give us back the church!

SEMINARY, ANYONE?

DEATH, ANYONE?

---

*Some such men were Priscillian, Columba, Peter Waldo, John Wycliffe, John Huss, William Tyndale, Konrad Grebel of the Swiss Anabaptists, Zinzendorf, Watchman Nee, Prem Pradham, and Bakht Singh.

ABOUT THE AUTHOR

Gene Edwards holds a B.A. from East Texas University, and a B.D. as well as an M.Div. from Southwestern Baptist Theological Seminary (1955), where he graduated at age 22. He is the author of over 30 books; some two million have been printed. His publishers are Zondervan, Random House, and Tyndale. Edwards is a frequent guest on national Christian television and Christian radio. His best-known books are *The Divine Romance*, *A Tale of Three Kings*, and *The Day I Was Crucified, as Told by Jesus Christ*. He has written five books dealing with suffering and pain. He pioneered and still belongs to the house church movement. He has been called *America's most loved Christian storyteller*.

During the early years of his ministry, Edwards was a pastor; and then, as an evangelist, he held city-wide campaigns sponsored by ministerial associations. He has been a frequent guest on TV and national Christian radio and a lecturer at seminaries and Bible schools throughout America as well as conference speaker on four continents. He and his wife make their home in Florida.

To contact the author, go to
geneedwards.com

Author Biography

Gene Edwards hold a B.A. from East Texas University, and a B.D. as well as an MDiv. from Southwestern Baptist Theological Seminary (1955), where he graduated at age 22. He is the author of over 30 books; some two million have been printed. His publishers are Zondervan, Random House, and Tyndale. He is a frequent guest on national Christian television and Christian radio. He and his wife make their home in Florida. His best-known books are *The Divine Romance, A Tale of Three Kings,* and *The Day I Was Crucified, as Told by Jesus Christ.* He pioneered and still belongs to the house church movement. He has been called *America's most loved Christian storyteller.*

During the early years of his ministry, Edwards was a pastor and then an evangelist. He held city-wide campaigns sponsored by ministerial associations. He has been a frequent guest on TV and national Christian radio and a lecturer at seminaries and Bible schools throughout America as well as conference speaker on four continents.

For more house church helps
or to
contact the author, go to
geneedwards.com
and click on
House Church Helps

ISSUES WE DARE NOT FACE

PAUL'S WAY OF TRAINING WORKERS
OR
THE SEMINARY'S WAY

Take a 2000-year-old journey through *seminary* history. You will discover that the origins of seminaries are not scriptural!

What you read here has never been written in a book, ever.

Why is it important for you to be interested in the seminary's origin and history? It is because ministers are trained in seminaries, which is a concept that, historically, evolved out of pagan education and reflects nothing of the way Jesus and Paul trained men.

You will then discover Paul's way of training workers. This, too, is a subject never before explored.

WHY DID WE PUBLISH THIS BOOK?

To reach men and women called of God, pointing them to a higher and better and far more scriptural way to be trained, and to reveal the *purpose* for being trained. These are issues never before faced.

You will also receive an excerpt from this book to share with others entitled *The Way Paul Trained Workers*. **$14.95**

THE SHOCKING STORY
OF THE
HISTORY OF *BIBLE STUDY*

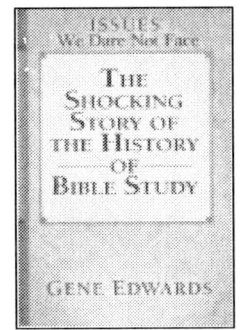

Who would ever think of such a subject. Once engaged, this book is not only shocking, but an eye-opener to the most basic problem in Christendom. We are studying the New Testament in a way that is untenable. This book reveals the wrong way and the best way to study the Scriptures. You may completely change the way you read your Bible, which in turn may change your life as it opens a way you never imagined for reading your Bible. **$14.95**

(Originally intended to be entitled *An Introduction to Revolutionary Bible Study*)

(Not the history of the Bible, but the history of Bible study)

ISSUES WE DARE NOT FACE

THE ORGANIC CHURCH VS THE "NEW TESTAMENT" CHURCH

The most sacred of all cows is now challenged ... the need of a "New Testament" church. Here is *the* New Testament church, *i.e.* the church that is organic. When the early churches were being formed, there was *no* New Testament in existence. What was emerging were churches which were organic to their very nature. Here is a new wrinkle on the evangelical brain—a totally new, better, and more scriptural way for the church to be born and to grow. The organic church, one that is wonderful, exciting and *natural* to God's people, and totally different to the way churches are raised up in modern times. There is a DNA of the church, and when she is raised up organically, she is a living creature, not a structure—the church spontaneous.

The reason for this book: to bring to us a totally new beginning for the body of Christ. **$9.95**

And Now to An Issue We Dare NOT Even Think About!!

WHY YOU SHOULD CONSIDER LEAVING THE PASTORATE

The Catholics must have a pope; we must have a pastor. It took the Reformation to show us that the pope was not in the New Testament.

In the years before the Reformation, the practice of the church's having a pope was *never* questioned. Today the practice of the pastorate is also never questioned. Here is an issue no one ever faces. The function of what a pastor does in carrying out the pastorate has no equivalent in Scripture.

This book does not make that fact the central issue. The issue is the incredible distraction that comes to a Christian called of God who is attempting to carry out this utterly nonscriptural task. Here is a book every pastor should read. It could liberate your life. For just one brief moment, you may want to consider that your call is not that of being called to the pastorate.

$8.95

HOUSE CHURCH HELPS

WHY SO MANY HOUSE CHURCHES FAIL
AND
WHAT TO DO ABOUT IT

$7.95

Here are forty years of church life experience that give workable answers. Everyone who has left the institutional church should read this book. The truth is, most house churches do fail. Why? The answer lies in how they begin. The author provides a fresh new departure from the *usual* way house churches begin. He then tells how to have a house church that will last.

PROBLEMS *AND* SOLUTIONS
IN
HOUSE CHURCHES

What are the problems in house churches? Why are Christians ill-equipped to deal with problems? Home churches have problems totally different from other churches. Here in this book you meet the unexpected problems—problems combined with practical solutions . . . which work. There is no theory or dreaming here. These are solutions which have stood the test of time. Expect to discover a whole new world of problems accompanied by solutions as unique and unexpected as the problems themselves.

$9.95

HOW TO START A HOUSE CHURCH FROM SCRATCH

$8.95

The first house church which was deliberately started in America was started by this author. Others followed. The reason these churches survive is because of the way they began. You will find the reason for their survival—unusual and unheard of—in the content of this audacious book. Everyone with an adventurous heart, looking for unusual answers, will enjoy reading this book.

House Church Movement

THESE BOOKS ARE LEADING THE WAY IN
A REVOLUTION IN THE PRACTICE OF CHURCH!

Beyond Radical
Gene Edwards

What if you found out that little we Protestants practice originates in the first century? The author describes where and how we got our present-day practices. He then calls us to move *Beyond Radical* to see true change in the church.

Read *Beyond Radical* only if you are seeking an alternative to Sunday morning services! This book could make a radical Christian out of you.

$7.⁹⁵

How to Meet in Homes
Gene Edwards

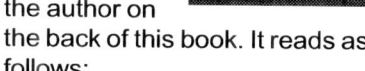

There is a warning from the author on the back of this book. It reads as follows:

This book is for those believers who want to utterly abandon it all, from top to bottom, and then start over in a way that is a revolutionary, radical departure from all present-day practices.

$11.⁹⁵

Revolution, the Story of the Early Church
Gene Edwards

A rip-roaring, hair-raising, edge-of-your-seat saga of the first-century believers. From the Day of Pentecost on, through the first seventeen years, every historical figure is there, alive, vivid, believable.

An historical cliffhanger written like a novel.

$11.⁹⁵

When the Church Was Led Only by Laymen
Gene Edwards

Edwards clearly reveals that throughout Scripture, it is the brothers and sisters who direct the church.

Discover your birthright . . . to function in a meeting of the body . . . not just sit in a pew as a spectator !

$5.⁰⁰

The First-Century Diaries

by
Gene Edwards

IF YOU NEVER READ ANY OTHER BOOKS ON THE NEW TESTAMENT . . . READ *THE FIRST-CENTURY DIARIES*!

Here is more than what you would learn in seminary! The Diaries will revolutionize your understanding of the New Testament, and, in turn will revolutionize your life. The best part is, this set of diaries reads like a novel. Never has learning the New Testament been so much fun.

The Silas Diary

This historical narrative parallels the book of Acts, giving a first-person account of Paul's first journey.

The Silas Diary is your invitation to join Silas, Paul, and their companions on a journey fraught with danger and adventure - a journey that changed the history of the world. Learn with the first-century Christians what freedom in Christ really means.

I.

The Titus Diary

This compelling narrative continues the events of the Book of Acts. *The Titus Diary* is a firsthand account of Paul's second journey as told by Titus.

Join this journey as Paul sets out once more-this time with Silas, Timothy, and Luke-and learn of the founding of the churches in Philippi, Thessalonica, Corinth, and Ephesus. Look on as Paul meets Aquila and Priscilla and quickly gains an appreciation of their passion for the Lord and his church.

II.

The First-Century Diaries

The Timothy Diary

In *The Timothy Diary* Paul's young Christian companion Timothy gives a firsthand account of Paul's third journey.

This journey is quite different from Paul's others. It is the fulfillment of Paul's dream, for in Ephesus Paul trains a handful of young men to take his place after his death. Paul follows Christ's example in choosing and training disciples to spread the gospel and encourage the growth of the church.

III.

The Priscilla Diary

Here are the stories of Paul's continued travels to the first-century churches narrated from the unique perspective of Priscilla, a vibrant first-century Christian woman!

See Paul writing his most personally revealing letter, his letter to the church in Corinth. Marvel at the truths Paul conveys to the church in Rome, a letter "of all that Paul considered central to the Christian life."

IV.

The Gaius Diary

Paul and Nero meet face to face in a moment of highest drama.

Paul is released, but soon is arrested again, and again faces Nero. The sentence is death. Just before his execution, all the men he trained arrived in Rome to be with him. *The Gaius Diary* gives life-changing insight into Paul's final letters. Colossians, Ephesians, Philemon, and Philippians come alive as you see in living color the background to these letters. Be there in April of 70 A.D. when Jerusalem is destroyed.

V.

For the first time ever in all church history, here is the entire first-century story from beginning to end.

The Chronicles of Heaven
by
Gene Edwards

The Old Testament

The Beginning covers *Genesis*, chapters 1&2 (*The Promise* will come next, covering the rest of *Genesis*). *The Escape*, already in print, covers *Exodus*. Other volumes will follow until the Pentateuch is finished.

In *The Beginning* God creates the heavens and the earth. The crowning glory of creation, man and woman, live and move in both the visible world and the spiritual world.

Experience one of the greatest events of human history: *The Escape* of the Israelite people from Egypt. Watch the drama from the view of earthly participants and the view of angels in the heavens.

Experience the wonderful story of the incarnation of Jesus, seen from both realms. *The Birth* introduces the mystery of the Christian life for those who have never heard the story.

The New Testament

The Chronicles then extend into the New Testament. They are *The Birth* and *The Triumph*. After *The Triumph* comes *The First-Century Diaries*!

In *The Triumph* you will experience the Easter story as you never have before. Join angels as they comprehend the suffering and death of Jesus and the mystery of free will in light of God's Eternal Purpose.

The Door has moved to a hill on Patmos. What would John be allowed to see? *The Return* invites you to witness the finale of the stirring conclusion to *The Chronicles of Heaven*.

AN INTRODUCTION TO
THE DEEPER CHRISTIAN LIFE
In Three Volumes
by
Gene Edwards

Living by the Highest Life

If you find yourself unsettled with Christianity as usual . . . if you find yourself longing for a deeper experience of the Christian life . . . *The Highest Life* is for you.

Did Jesus Christ live the Christian life merely by human effort? Or did Jesus understand living by the Spirit— —His Father's Life in Him?

Discover what it means to live a spiritual life while living on earth.

I.

The Secret to the Christian Life

Read the Bible, pray, go to church, tithe . . . is this what it means to live the Christian life? Is there more to living the Christian life than following a set of rules? How did Jesus live by the Spirit?

The Secret to the Christian Life reveals the one central secret to living out the Christian life. Nor does the book stop there . . . it also gives *practical* ways to enhance your fellowship with the Lord.

II.

The Inward Journey

The Inward Journey is the companion volume to *The Secret to the Christian Life*. A beautiful story of a dying uncle explaining to his nephew, a new Christian, the ways and mysteries of the cross and of suffering. Of those who have a favorite Gene Edwards book, tens of thousands have selected *The Inward Journey* as that book.

III.

The Divine Romance
by
Gene Edwards

The Divine Romance is praised as one of the all-time literary achievements of the Protestant era. Breathtakingly beautiful, here is the odyssey of Christ's quest for His bride. *The Divine Romance* is the most captivating, heartwarming and inspirational romance, transcending space and time. In all of Christian literature there has never been a description of the crucifixion and resurrection which so rivals the one depicted in *The Divine Romance*.

Many readers have commented, "This book should come with a box of Kleenex." The description of the romance between Adam and Eve alone is one of the great love stories of all times.

Edwards' portrayal of the romance of Christ and His bride takes its place along side such classics as Dante's *The Divine Comedy* and Milton's *Paradise Lost*. Reading this literary masterpiece will alter your life forever.

One of the greatest Christian classics of all time.

SeedSowers Publishing House
P.O. Box 3317
Jacksonville, FL 32206
800-228-2665   seedsowers.com

THE NEW TESTAMENT
IN FIRST PERSON

THE STORY OF MY LIFE
AS TOLD BY JESUS CHRIST

Listen to Jesus, the Christ, tell His own story... in His own words... to you!

All four Gospels have been combined in one single, flowing narrative. And it is in the first person! The Story of My Life as Told by Jesus Christ is a complete and thorough account of the events of Christ's life. Now you can read all of the Lord's life in chronological order, without repetition of a single detail. Every sentence in the Gospels is included, plus times, dates and places.

Allow yourself to be immersed into the setting of the life and ministry of Christ. Follow His footsteps as He walked the earth with those He knew and loved, in one smooth, flowing, uninterrupted story.

The impact is so arresting you will feel that you are hearing the gospel story for the first time. And always, in first person, the Lord is speaking directly to you. Think of it as The Jesus Diary.

ACTS IN FIRST PERSON

For the first time in history, you can read the Acts of the Apostles in first person... like a diary.

Listen to the men who lived during the exciting early years of the church. Experience the excitement and danger as these men travel to declare Jesus Christ. Every detail is included... such as dates and location.

Based on Tyndale's New Living Translation Bible, *Acts in First Person* is in readable, contemporary English. A wonderful study aid for all ages.

SEEDSOWERS
800-228-2665 (fax) 866-252-5504
www.seedsowers.com

REVOLUTIONARY BOOKS ON CHURCH LIFE

Beyond Radical *(Edwards)*	7.95
How to Meet in Homes *(Edwards)*	10.95
An Open Letter to House Church Leaders *(Edwards)*	5.00
When the Church Was Led Only by Laymen *(Edwards)*	5.00
Revolution, The Story of the Early Church *(Edwards)*	11.95
The Silas Diary *(Edwards)*	9.99
The Titus Diary *(Edwards)*	8.99
The Timothy Diary *(Edwards)*	9.99
The Priscilla Diary *(Edwards)*	9.99
The Gaius Diary *(Edwards)*	10.99
Overlooked Christianity *(Edwards)*	10.95
Paul's Way of Training Workers or the Seminary's Way *(Edwards)*	14.95
The Shocking Story of the History of Bible Study *(Edwards)*	14.95
Why You Should Consider Leaving the Pastorate *(Edwards)*	8.95
The Organic Church vs. the "New Testament" Church *(Edwards)*	9.95
Problems and Solutions in House Churches *(Edwards)*	9.95
How to Start a House Church from Scratch *(Edwards)*	8.95
Why So Many House Churches Fail and What to Do about It *(Edwards)*	7.95

AN INTRODUCTION TO THE DEEPER CHRISTIAN LIFE

Living by the Highest Life *(Edwards)*	10.99
The Secret to the Christian Life *(Edwards)*	9.99
The Inward Journey *(Edwards)*	10.99

CLASSICS ON THE DEEPER CHRISTIAN LIFE

Experiencing the Depths of Jesus Christ *(Guyon)*	9.95
Practicing His Presence *(Lawrence/Laubach)*	9.95
The Spiritual Guide *(Molinos)*	9.95
Union with God *(Guyon)*	8.95
The Seeking Heart *(Fenelon)*	9.95
Intimacy with Christ *(Guyon)*	10.95
Spiritual Torrents *(Guyon)*	10.95
The Ultimate Intention *(Fromke)*	10.00
One Hundred Days in the Secret Place *(Edwards)*	12.99

IN A CLASS BY ITSELF

The Divine Romance *(Edwards)*	11.99

NEW TESTAMENT

The Story of My Life as Told by Jesus Christ *(Four Gospels blended)*	14.95
The Day I was Crucified as Told by Jesus the Christ	14.99
Acts in First Person *(Book of Acts)*	9.95

COMMENTARIES BY JEANNE GUYON

Genesis	10.95
Exodus	10.95
Leviticus - Numbers - Deuteronomy	12.95
Judges	7.95
Job	10.95
Song of Songs *(Song of Solomon Commentary)*	9.95

(Prices subject to change)

COMMENTARIES BY JEANNE GUYON *(Continued)*
Jeremiah Commentary 7.95
James - I John - Revelation Commentaries 12.95

THE CHRONICLES OF HEAVEN *(Edwards)*
Christ Before Creation 8.99
The Beginning 8.99
The Escape 8.99
The Birth 8.99
The Triumph 8.99
The Return 8.99

THE COLLECTED WORKS OF T. AUSTIN-SPARKS
The Centrality of Jesus Christ 19.95
The House of God 29.95
Ministry 29.95
Service 19.95
Spiritual Foundations 29.95
The Things of the Spirit 10.95
Prayer 14.95
The On-High Calling 10.95
Rivers of Living Water 8.95
The Power of His Resurrection 8.95

COMFORT AND HEALING
A Tale of Three Kings *(Edwards)* 8.99
The Prisoner in the Third Cell *(Edwards)* 9.99
Letters to a Devastated Christian *(Edwards)* 7.95
Exquisite Agony *(Edwards)* 9.95
Dear Lillian *(Edwards)* paperback 5.95
Dear Lillian *(Edwards)* hardcover 9.99

OTHER BOOKS ON CHURCH LIFE
Climb the Highest Mountain *(Edwards)* 12.95
The Torch of the Testimony *(Kennedy)* 14.95
The Passing of the Torch *(Chen)* 9.95
Going to Church in the First Century *(Banks)* 5.95
When the Church Was Young *(Loosley)* 8.95
Church Unity *(Litzman,Nee,Edwards)* 10.95
Let's Return to Christian Unity *(Kurosaki)* 10.95

CHRISTIAN LIVING
The Christian Woman . . . Set Free *(Edwards)* 12.95
Your Lord Is a Blue Collar Worker *(Edwards)* 7.95
The Autobiography of Jeanne Guyon 19.95
Final Steps in Christian Maturity *(Guyon)* 12.95
Turkeys and Eagles *(Lord)* 9.95
The Life of Jeanne Guyon *(T.C. Upham)* 17.95
Life's Ultimate Privilege *(Fromke)* 10.00
Unto Full Stature *(Fromke)* 10.00
All and Only *(Kilpatrick)* 8.95
Adoration *(Kilpatrick)* 9.95
Release of the Spirit *(Nee)* 9.99
Bone of His Bone *(Huegel)* modernized 9.95
You Can Witness with Confidence *(Rinker)* 10.95